SALVATION
DEPICTED IN A MEAL

*An Hebraic Christian
Guide to Passover
(Non Traditional)*

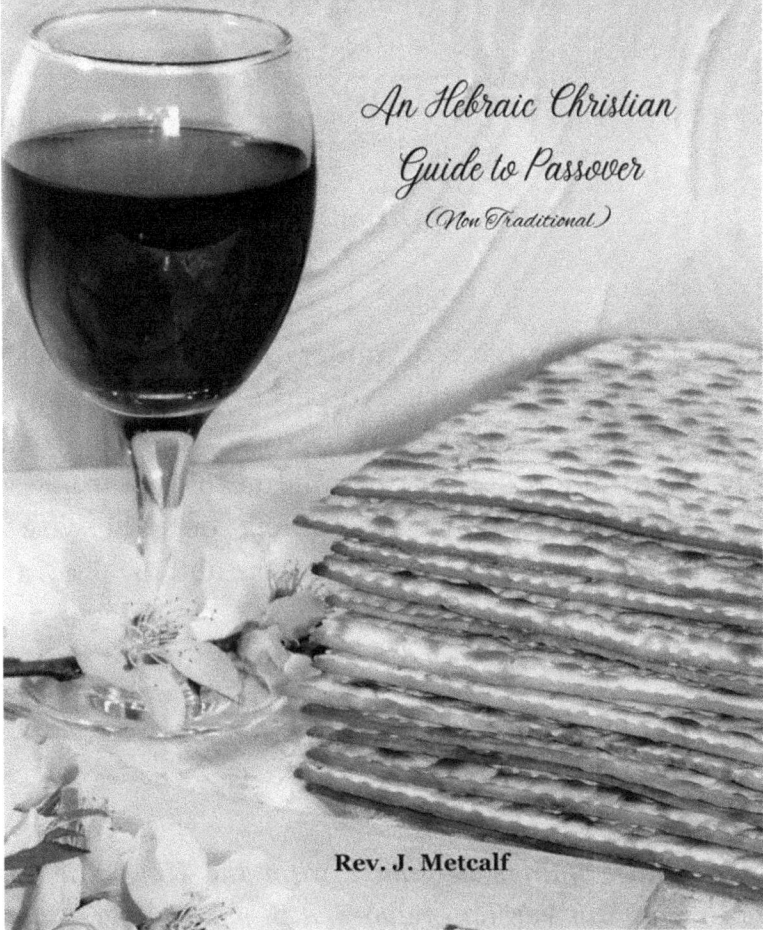

Rev. J. Metcalf

1st Printing 2014
Format Revised 2024
Cegullah Publishing & Apologetics Academy
Copyright 2024
www.cegullahpublishing.ca
All rights reserved.

Cegullah Publishing &
סְגֻלָּה
Treasures
in Print
Apologetics Academy

ISBN # 978-0-9813194-0-7

All scripture quotes originate from the King James Public Domain Version, reworded in many places, by the author, into modern English.

INDEX

Introduction   7

PRELIMINARIES FOR PASSOVER MEAL

As Guests Arrive   28

Leader Overview   27

Meal Divisions   11

Pre-Celebration Instructions   24

Preliminaries After Guests are Seated   29

Recipe for Charoset   23

Suggestions for Picking Leaders   25

Table Setting   12

PASSOVER CELEBRATION (Part 1)

Greens Dipped in Saltwater   50

Lighting the Candle   33

Partake of Lamb   75

Shofar Blow   30

Thanksgiving for Main Meal   81

The 4 Questions   55

The Cup of Judgment   67

Ten Commandments   71

The Kiddish Cup   36

Washing the Hands   78

PASSOVER CELEBRATION (Part 2)

Elijah's Coming   85

Final Instructions and Closing   105

The Bread of Redemption   86

The Cup of Praise, (Introduction)   91

The Cup of Praise   101

The Cup of Redemption   89

The Great Hallel (Introduction)   92

SECTION I

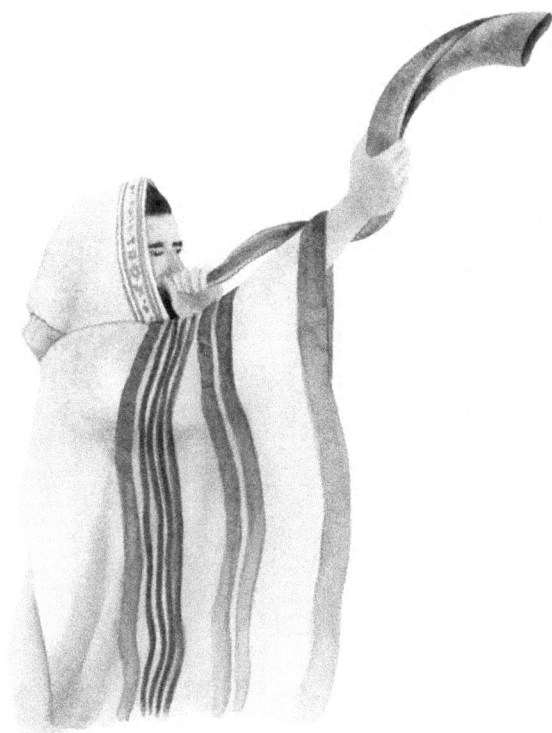

PRELIMINARIES FOR PASSOVER MEAL

INTRODUCTION

More and more Christian believers, all over the world, make a definite decision to explore the ancients roots of the Christian faith. When they do, they soon discover many prophetic pictures or foreshadows of Yeshua, hidden within the Hebraic Scriptures. They find too, that the Feasts of the LORD, when understood in light of the New Testament, hold many marvellous truths about Yeshua.

Since these Feasts so clearly depict Yeshua within them, many believers choose to celebrate the Feasts. For believers with a Gentile background, this decision brings with it certain challenges since most are not sure how to celebrate the feasts properly. To look at the Jewish traditions of the feasts, as a model, poses a problem since that expression of the feasts often include Rabbinical or legalistic traditions, which Christians prefer to exclude. Thus, many believers, not certain of the details to include or exclude in their celebration of the feasts, need some assistance to show them what to do.

This is the purpose of this guide: to assist believers in Yeshua to celebrate the Passover, scripturally, confidently, and comfortably within their own home, or within a church setting.

"Salvation Depicted in a Meal" clearly shows Yeshua within the Passover. It presents a New Testament understanding of His role as the Passover Lamb, and as the fulfilment of that Feast. Looking then, at the Passover in this light, believers reinforce their Christian faith, and at the same time, if they so desire, they use this feast as an opportunity to invite family and friends to join them. Doing this brings the gospel message to others in a very family like environment. Perhaps, for some guests, this may be the first time they hear the gospel message of salvation.

We trust, as you use "Salvation Depicted in a Meal", you will have a Passover Celebration that is delightful, meaningful, rewarding and honouring to God.

THE HAGGADAH

Traditionally, the Jews call the guide to the Passover Celebration a "Haggadah', which means, "the Telling". The Haggadah tells the story of the Passover and contains the appropriate dialogue throughout the meal. The eldest, male member of the family usually presides over the meal. Meal attendees, especially children, participate as much as possible, so that all learn about the Passover. Each person sitting at the table, that is old enough to read, follows along from the Haggadah, giving each person opportunity to gain a full understanding of the Passover Meal.

THIS HAGGADAH OVERVIEW

This Haggadah holds the specific dialogue for an Hebraic Christian celebration of the Passover Meal. It outlines each different aspect of the Passover Meal "telling" how it represents Yeshua. It includes prayers, worded in the first person, to make the experience personally applicable, and with that personal application in mind, the prayers are worded in English, not Hebrew, since few Gentile believers in Yeshua are fluent in Hebrew. These prayers, while they hold to some basics of the Hebrew wording, reflect the New Covenant interpretation of the Passover, and therefore, remain non-traditional when compared to prayers said in most Jewish Passover celebrations.

Since the Passover Meal contains much dialogue, and since participation within the Passover is important, we distribute the dialogue amongst four leaders. We chose that number because of the four Cups used at Passover and therefore each leader has a turn in leading the Passover guests in partaking of one specific Cup.

You may prefer to separate the dialogue into more parts, or perhaps fewer, depending on the guests you have at your Passover Meal. Whatever you chose to do, remember to enjoy the rich imagery of Yeshua; reverentially partake of each aspect within the meal and rejoice in the finished works of the Lamb of God, who provided salvation for you at the cross of Calvary.

Experience your celebration of the Passover, depicting Yeshua as the Passover Lamb.

HONOURING THE NAME OF GOD

Most Jews today do not say the name of the LORD, but rather substitute it with Ha Shem, meaning The Name, or Adonai, meaning Lord. However, we suggest that wherever possible when reading this book for Passover and you see the writing, "the LORD", you substitute and pronounce it with the first covenant name of God, namely, YeHoVaH.

To honour the Jewishness of Jesus, we also use the Name, Yeshua and invite you to do the same. [1]

---

[1] [1] Nehemiah Gordon, a Hebrew scholar, according to his testimony, found the name of the Father with all vowel pointings in the Aleppo Codex, and through his efforts, and those of others discovered that name with vowel pointings in over 2000 manuscripts. For more information on Nehemiah Gordon, enter his name in a browser or visit nehemiaswall.com.

MEAL DIVISIONS

It works best to divide the Passover Meal into four main divisions:

First 2 cups:	This part of the celebration takes about 1 hour. It explains the Kiddish Cup, the unleavened bread, the use of the bitter herb and the bitter-sweet herb, the cup of Judgment and concludes with hand washing, prior to serving the main meal.
Main Meal	Give your guests lots of time to enjoy this meal and each other. This gives lots of time to enjoy the food and each other[2], and to take a washroom break before resuming.
Last 2 Cups	This part of the celebration takes between 45 to 60 minutes and includes the mention of Elijah, the Bread and Cup of Redemption, and the Cup of Praise. It also includes the Great Hallel, which is an inclusion of scripture reading Yeshua most likely

---

[2] If you wish to obtain recipes for Jewish dishes to serve during this time of the Passover Meal, there are numerous recipes on the internet. If you prefer to serve the traditional food of your country, *try to use recipes without yeast,* as the absence of yeast represents the absence of sin in Yeshua's life.

11

	recited, probably some of it at the end of the Passover, and some on the way to the Garden of Gethsemane.
Ending	Close the celebration with prayer and afterwards invite your guests to relax and stay awhile. In Israel, due to their pleasant weather, some Passover celebrations include singing around a campfire. Others prefer to retire to a living room setting where guests can continue to fellowship or pray one for another. Provide whatever you feel is best for your guests and personal Passover setting.

TABLE SETTING

A well-organized Passover Meal runs smoothly. To facilitate this, prepare your table well ahead of time, long before the guests arrive. You will find a recap of the items needed to celebrate the Passover Meal right below this paragraph. Please Note: Many people use traditional Jewish serving dishes for the various parts of the Meal; however, this is not a necessity. Use whatever dishes you have available[3].

---

[3] If you wish to purchase some small, inexpensive dishes that will accommodate some Passover items such as the herbs or parsley, you might find it helpful, but it is not necessary.

FOOD & BEVERAGE

- Matzah bread[4]. Each person will need enough Matzah to take in their hands and break into 2 pieces
- Bitter herb[5]
- Bittersweet herb called Charoset, pronounced (kha-roh-set)[6]
- water with salt added to represent tears[7]
- parsley
- non-alcoholic wine (or grape juice)[8]
- Small pieces of cooked lamb (these small pieces of lamb must be available for the part

---

[4] This is unleavened bread. Speciality grocery stores usually carry this bread. We suggest you use unleavened bread at this meal, as it represents Yeshua's sinless life. Some people prefer those desserts, served at the meal, do not contain yeast.

[5] Most common bitter herb used is Horseradish.

[6] This dip is made from apples. We have included a recipe.

[7] Make your own saline solution. Place it in small bowls on the table, near the parsley bowls.

[8] Non-alcoholic wine verse alcoholic wine many Christians discuss. If you chose to use alcoholic wine, remember there are four cups of wine served at Passover. Since, in some people, intoxication happens easily, use caution and care in the size of cups you use, especially if you desire your guests to drink the entire cup of wine for the four cups in Passover. A suggestion might be to serve communion size cups. Whatever you chose to use, as a good host, be sure to advise your guests ahead of time regarding the cups of wine to drink. ***Ensure your guests are sober before returning to their cars to drive home.***

of the Passover that transpires, pre-meal. (See section Partake of the Lamb.)

For the full course meal, ensure you have the food you need to accommodate your guests. Prepare it ahead of time but gear it to be ready about 1 hour into the celebration.

Passover Dishes

- plates for Matzah
- 4 bowls: 1 each for parsley, salt water, bitter herb and Charoset
- cups to hold wine/grape juice
- dessert plate to hold drops of wine during 1st Division of the Passover[9]

Bread and Desserts

Typically, the Bible commands that this feast be celebrated without yeast in the bread or desserts. This absence of yeast, in Israel, goes on for 40 days after the Passover and the Jews count the Omer. To honour God and the fact that He removed sin in your life, consider abstaining from using yeast in your bread and desserts for the Passover celebration.

---

[9] Later, the guests take their finger, dip in the wine, and put a drop on the dessert plate, remembering the 10 commandments given at Mt. Sinai.

Dinner Dishes

In a Jewish home, special dishes are kept aside and only used at Passover. While this is not necessary, in giving your best, you honour the Lord[10].

Each person will need:

- 1 Wine goblet, silver, or glass[11] (some use 4 separate cups per guest[12])
- 1 dinner plate
- 1 small plate to put in wine drops as we say the 10 commandments
- 1 small napkin (to wipe wine from fingers after remembering 10 commandments)
- Dinner cutlery
- Dinner napkin

This is what you need *per guest*. When you count your guests, *consider adding to the number a plate setting and a cup for Elijah*, as this is a custom of the Jews to expect Elijah to come to the Passover (see below about Elijah).

NOTE: Some prefer not to set the table for dinner use when they begin the Passover celebration but rather just put on the table what you need for the first half of the Passover meal.

---

[10] Having said that, some people prefer to use a good quality of disposable plates which look like china, as well as matching silver. As a rule of thumb, use whatever you believe honours God.

[11] For very young children, you may prefer to use something unbreakable and more suitable for them to hold.

[12] If you wish to use 4 cups per person, to save on table space, consider using small 1-ounce cups.

Tablecloth

Use your best tablecloth if you can. Some use white, while others prefer blue or other colours. If your table is wide enough, you might wish to use a runner with a Passover theme in the centre of the table.

Elijah's cup

Traditionally, Jews place a cup at the table for Elijah. If you decide to do this, do so with this scripture in mind: *Malachi 4: 5 "Behold, I will send you Elijah the prophet before the coming of the great and dreadful day of the LORD: 6 And he shall turn the heart of the fathers to the children, and the heart of the children to their fathers, lest I come and smite the earth with a curse."*[13] You might consider placing a card with this scripture nearby so your guests will understand the cup's purpose.

Menorah/Candles

Menorahs are readily available on the internet or at some Jewish stores in the larger cities. When using a Menorah, please note there are 2 types of Menorahs available.

- The 7-branch Menorah
- The 9 branch Menorah

---

[13] Believers can use this opportunity to speak about the 2nd Coming of Yeshua!

Use the 7 branch Menorah on Passover.
Use the 9-branch Menorah on Hanukkah.

If you do not own a Menorah, use one or more single candles to light for this Passover Meal.

CAUTION: Whatever you use, place your candles with fire safety in mind. Ensure your guests, especially small children, cannot easily knock them over. Ensure all candles are in proper candleholders, and not near anything flammable such as curtains, wall hangings, etc.

Other Items
If your dishes and tablecloth are both white, you might wish to use coloured chargers, placemats, or something to help the dishes stand out. Use whatever you like to make the table look special, different than normal and thus, appropriate for this special occasion.

Afikomen:
This use of an afikomen is not specifically written in the Bible, therefore, in this Haggadah, we do not use the Afikomen, however, many prefer to incorporate its use especially when young children are present. If this is your preference, to use it basically requires a napkin and piece of matzah bread. You break the matzah bread and wrap a portion of the bread in a napkin, then hide the wrapped bread somewhere in the house. Later, the children search to find it. When they do, they

receive a reward. If you wish to learn more, the internet has many explanations of its use and timing in the Passover Meal.

ADDITIONAL COMMENTS

Children	Position the children as close as possible to an adult in case the child needs assistance during the meal with things such as breaking matzah bread dipping in the herbs etc. It is important to allow children to partake in this meal as much as possible. Traditionally, the children ask the questions at the meal (see section on 4 Questions). If you wish to implement that aspect, be sure to inform the leader(s) handling the questions so they can cue or help the child to ask the question. Ensure you invite your guests well ahead of time so they can look forward to this very important day in their life.
Guests	To include your guests more in the Passover Celebration, you might consider asking them to think of themselves as travellers on a journey to another country and thus, bring with them one item they absolutely must have if they were asked to leave their

present country for another. At the meal's end give them time to share what they brought and why they brought it. This makes the meal more personal and makes for an interesting time of sharing.

What to Avoid

Avoid large displays of flowers in tall vases which obscure guests from easily looking at each other.

Music, if used at all, should complement the theme of Passover, and play softly in the background.

Please avoid last minute preparations. Be prepared well ahead of time as this makes your Passover meal flow more smoothly.

A Special note: In consideration of guests who may have **allergies** or **sensitivities to certain smells or foods,** check with your guests to ensure the food served does not cause problems for those with allergies.

If you do this Passover in a larger setting with many guests you might not know personally, such as in a church setting, consider using *scent-free candles and if possible, ask your guests not to wear perfume.* It is a little harder to personally ask about allergies to foods in a bigger setting, so be sure to have some form of protocol in place to check for food allergies.

Closing	Decide ahead of time how you plan to close the Passover gathering. Many people use dessert as a time to close and sit around and share testimonies, or other such things which build faith and make for good fellowship.

A TABLE READY FOR PASSOVER

3 dishes in the centre are smaller ones used to hold the charoset, salt water, & bitter herb (horse radish)

The picture shows part of a Passover table setting. As you can see by looking at the picture, we provided a dinner plate, a dessert plate *(placed inside the dinner plate)*, knife, forks, spoon, napkins, wine goblet, and place card for each guest. In front of the placemat, you see three small white dishes. The first dish *(near the place card)* holds bitter herbs, the centre dish holds salt water, and the third dish contains Charoset. These 2" square dishes are shared between two people, however, that is not necessary[14]. Since we have a lot of

---

[14] You may wish to place these dishes differently or use larger dishes and have your guests pass the dishes to each other.

guests, we find this saves time to have items closer and ready for use.

The tall, clear dish behind the Charoset is empty in the picture, but during the Passover it contains parsley. The top right-hand side of the picture shows another side dish where we placed the Matzah.

Regarding the small dessert plate placed inside the dinner plate, it is there to hold 10 tiny drops of wine that, at one point in the meal, each participant places o that dessert plate to represent the commandments given at Mount Sinai. We use the small white napkin to wipe the fingers after that part of the Celebration. The larger dinner napkins, beneath the forks, are for use during the meal.

Please note, in the centre of the table, the candles (scent free) are encased in glass. When lit, the flame comes beneath the rim of the glass container[15].

---

[15] As a personal preference, we like to use small barbecue lighters to light the candle, hence the lighter seen on the small plate near the top, left hand side of the picture. Sometimes, we have used small, battery powered mini lights that sit on top of the menorah, or candle holders.

RECEIPE FOR CHAROSET[16]

INGREDIENTS
- 6 apples, peeled & cored (some like Fuji apples)
- 1cup finely chopped walnuts
- 2 teaspoons cinnamon (some prefer less)
- 3 ½ teaspoons of honey
- 1/3 cup of grape juice

DIRECTIONS
- Chop apples with a food processor[17]
- Put into a large bowl
- Add honey, grape juice and cinnamon
- Keep refrigerated until needed
-

Place into small bowls on the table for use

---

[16] ***This recipe includes nuts and cinnamon***. Be sure your guests are not allergic to nuts or cinnamon. If so, omit the nuts and use your favourite substitute for cinnamon.

[17] When preparing for special company, some people become flustered, especially when doing something for the first time. So, just a reminder here, not to take short cuts but give yourself plenty of time in preparing the food. Use safety habits when cooking, or when using your food processor and other such items which can cause injury. Also, *please note* that some people prefer *to cook the apples until they are tender*. Some people, with small children, prefer to puree the apples. Should you **not** want this recipe, there are many others easily found on the internet or in a local library. Just remember the name Charoset when you do your research, as that will make it easier to locate what you desire.

PRE-CELEBRATION INSTRUCTIONS

1. Be sure you give yourself lots of time to prepare for the Passover. Read the guide over carefully noting, beforehand, the preparations of food needed. Don't forget the special items such as Charoset, bitter herbs[18], parsley and salt water, and small pieces of lamb available before the meal. (See section Partake of the Lamb.)

2. Choose your leaders long beforehand & ensure they receive a leader's guide well ahead of time to become familiar with their part.

3. Get your table ready with all the necessary dishes for the 1st part of the Passover Celebration. The more you prepare beforehand, the easier things flow during the Passover Meal.

4. Ensure you have pitcher, bowl, & towels available for hand washing[19].

---

[18] Some use horseradish.

[19] Using disposable towel or towelettes work well, also, and of course, are very sanitary.

SUGGESTIONS FOR PICKING LEADERS

Choosing leaders:
Even those this guide sets our four leaders; four leaders are not a necessity. In this Passover feast, incorporating more than one leader helps to involve more people in the Passover. How you decide to do the Passover, is up to do. Four leaders are a suggestion. Perhaps, you may prefer one person to do it all, and as they go along, they assign parts to others. Or maybe you prefer to divide the reading portions into eight parts. Do whatever suits your circumstances and need the best.

Whatever you decide, here are a few suggestions for choosing leaders:
1. Read through the "Leader Overview" following this information. This gives you a better idea as to the part of each leader.
2. Choose your leader with their responsibilities in mind.

After choosing your leaders or even when you ask them to take part in the Passover, be sure they have a guide either at the time of your asking, or well ahead of time before the Passover celebration so they can familiarize themselves with their part. This helps with their comfortability and makes the celebration run smoothly.

Please note in every division of the meal, all four leaders have a part to read aloud.

Some thoughts to consider in choosing leaders:

1. **Leader # 1:** in a home environment is usually the father. If this is not possible, another person, such as the mother, the oldest son, oldest daughter, or a respected friend of the family can also lead. In a church setting, the pastor, deacon, or any capable person can lead[20].

2. **Leaders # 2, # 3 and # 4:** These leaders should be old enough to read their part and able to speak well enough to be heard[21].

3. Place Leaders at the table where they can be easily seen and heard. If in a larger setting, a sound system should be used wherever possible.

---

[20] We find dispersing the leader roles among our guests gives opportunity for more involvement by others as well as builds confidence for guests to do their own Passover in following years. Also, since we are familiar with all parts, if someone is needed at the last minute, we are on standby to fill in.

[21] Roles in this Haggadah are not gender or age specific. In a family setting, young children, if they can read, can take a minimal or full part, adding adult assistance where needed.

LEADER OVERVIEW

Leader # 1

Shofar Blow	30
Lighting the Candle, Opening	33
Lighting the Candle, Declaration	35
Question 1	56
Matzah Bread Thanksgiving	57
Washing Hands Instructions	78
Thanking God & Meal Instructions	81
Elijah's Coming	85
Cup of Redemption Declaration	90
Cup of Praise Introduction	91
Great Hallel Introduction	92
Sinner's Prayer	103
Final Instructions and Closing	105

Leader # 2

Question # 2	58
Bitter Herb Thanksgiving	61
Partake of Lamb Declaration	77
Cup of Praise Declaration	101

Leader # 3

Greens Dipped in Saltwater Declaration	53
Question # 3	61
Bittersweet Herb Thanksgiving	63
Ten Commandments	71
Cup of Judgment Declaration	74

Leader # 4

Kiddish Cup Declarations	49
Question # 4	63
Rest Admonition	66
Bread of Redemption Declaration	88

There are many prayers said during the Passover Meal. It works best if each person has a guide to follow along, as that ensures the best possible participation in the meal. If each participant does not have a guide, ensure the leader speaks the prayer, bit by bit, so all can follow along and thus participate that way.

As Guests Arrive

If you prefer, before the Passover Celebration begins, ask for volunteers that, upon the leaders cue, will do one of the following:

- light the candle (or candles on their table)
- speak the declaration based on John 8:12 during the opening part of the Passover Celebration, and
- ensure juice[22] is in the cups *before* they are needed, at any time during the meal.

---

[22] For various reasons, some believers prefer non-alcoholic wine, however, if you prefer to use alcoholic wine, you do not wish to cause any problems with your guests drinking too much, especially, if they need to drive home later. Do consider limiting the size of the cups since there are 4 Passover cups from which to drink. Take good care of your guests. Surely, God desires you to be a responsible host and blesses you for you care of others.

PRELIMINARIES AFTER GUESTS ARE SEATED

Leader # 1   (Or Host or Hostess)

- Seat your guests.
- Open this Passover Meal with a warm, friendly welcome to those present. Remind them that Passover is an appointed time ("moedim"[23], in Hebrew), a time when God promises that He meets with His People. While He is with us always, some of your guests might not be saved and this fact may be important to them.
- Help your guests to understand the Passover Meal by introducing the Haggadah to your guests, explaining how it will be used throughout the Passover Celebration. (If each guest will not have a Haggadah, explain how they are to follow the Celebration order.) No matter how you decide to handle the instructions, ensure that your guests are clear on how to proceed, so they can enjoy the experience of Passover.
- (If you use alcoholic wine, this is a good place to mention the number of cups to drink as a caution to be careful).
- Pray for your guests.

---

[23] Pronounced "mow-a-dee-uhm".

SHOFAR BLOW[24]

To open with a shofar blow consider using *any* of the following, or your own variation:

- Leader # 1 blows the shofar.
- Any leader blows the shofar.
- Two of three people blow a shofar together in unison.
- All guests who own shofars blow the shofar together, in unison.
- Use a prerecorded shofar blow.

Whatever you chose, pre-arrange this before the Passover gathering and practise if necessary.

Have the shofar blow either *before or after* the opening prayer, whichever is your preference. As this shofar blow signals the beginning of your Passover gathering, those who own a tallit might wish to don it at this time. Invite them to do so!

---

[24] The shofar is an animal horn, symbolic of redemption. It is wonderful to use a shofar blow as it is very Jewish and customary at feasts. However, if you do not have one, you can substitute with a trumpet blow, or find a recording. If you can't find anything, you can omit this and then move on.

SECTION 2

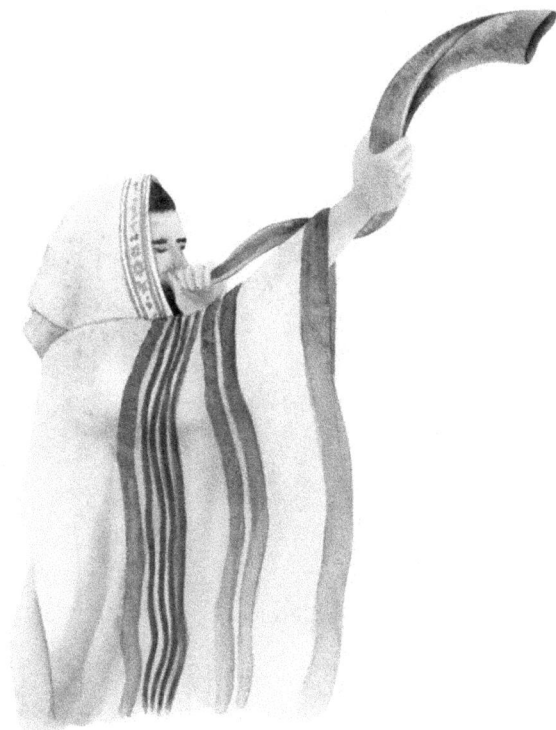

PASSOVER
CELEBRATION
(Part 1)

PASSOVER OPENING

Put on tallits, etc. and open with shofar blow.

LIGHTING OF THE CANDLE

Leader # 1

This night is about Yeshua.

- He is God's Passover Lamb and tonight we gather to honour Him, and to celebrate what He has done on behalf of all human beings, and more specifically, *what He has done for you and for me.*

Leader # 2:

This Passover meal is about Yeshua.

- Scripture calls Yeshua the Last Adam
- There was, however, a *first* Adam. This Adam was spoken of in Genesis, in the Garden of Eden. He is the father of all humankind.
- One day, the first Adam disobeyed God.

- When Adam disobeyed God, sin entered the world and with it, death.
- In God's eyes, every human being, even though yet unborn, lived within Adam, the father of all humanity.
- Therefore, when Adam sinned, all humankind sinned, and consequently, death comes to all.
- That might sound strange but, according to the Bible, that is how God sees it.

Leader # 3:

- Yeshua, however, was born of a virgin, of a woman's seed.
- Therefore, He was not born of the seed of the first Adam, and thus, was born without sin and the penalty of death.
- Yeshua lived His whole life on earth, without sin and thus, in God's eyes, lived one hundred percent in righteousness.
- Yeshua, therefore, God considered a spotless Lamb; **one without blemish.**

Leader # 4:

- Yeshua, God's Perfect Lamb, is also called, "The Light of the World".
- Without His Light, all humankind lives in darkness.

- Yeshua came to earth so that all who live in darkness would see His marvellous light and hopefully, be drawn to Him.
- All those who come to Him and believe in Him walk in the light and have the light of life.
- To show Yeshua as the Light of the World and His powerful influence in it, we light a candle and make a declaration.

Leader # 1:

- I will give instructions first.
- Who has been asked to light the candles?
- On my signal, you light the candles.
- After doing so, you can sit down again, and we will say the scripture, together.

- All who are going to light the candles, please stand.
- Take the light in your hand.
- Light the candles now, please.
- Thank you. Please sit down again.
- Let's declare this scripture together:

ALL: "Yeshua said, "I am the Light of the World: whosoever follows Me shall not walk in darkness, but they shall have the light of life."

THE KIDDISH CUP
(CUP OF SANCTIFICATION)

Leader # 1 continues.

There are 4 cups we will drink during the Passover Meal:

- These 4 cups come from Exodus 6:6-7
- Each cup recaptures the *"I will"* of this scripture passage.
- **Cup 1: The Kiddish Cup**[25]: *"I will bring you* out from under the burdens of the Egyptians".
- **Cup 2: The Cup of Judgment**: *"I will* free you from Egyptian bondage".
- **Cup 3: The Cup of Redemption**: *"I will* redeem you with a stretched-out arm, & with great judgments".
- **Cup 4 The Cup of Praise**: *"And I will* receive you as My people, and I will be your God".

---

[25] Pronounced Kid-dish.

- In this first part of our celebration of the Passover, we drink the Kiddish cup, *the cup which spoke of Israel's coming out of Egypt*, but due to Messiah's coming, this cup speaks so much more to those who believe Yeshua was that long awaited Messiah.
- The word "Kiddish" comes from the Hebrew word, "Kadosh"[26], which translates as "holy", sanctified, set apart, separated unto God alone.
- Before we drink of this cup, to understand more about it, we'll look back to the first Passover when God brought His people out of the land of Egypt.

Leader # 2:

- Israel, at one time, was a nation living within another nation, the nation of Egypt.
- Israel, once their numbers grew, were feared by the Egyptians, and so their Pharoah decided to make the nation of Israel a subservient nation within Egypt. In other words, Pharoah enslaved the Israelites.
- Pharoah became a tyrant over Israel, and thus, Israel received treatment by the government and the rulers of Egypt.

---

[26] Pronounced "kah- dosh".

- Pharaoh kept the Israelites in utter poverty and treated them dreadfully.
- After a period of four hundred and thirty years of the children of Israel in Egypt, God determined that the time had come for Israel to leave Egypt and become the free nation that He desired them to be.
- For that to happened, Pharaoh, the head of Egyptian government, must release God's People.
- God sent a man named Moses to speak this command to Pharoah:

"Let My People go"

ALL: **Let My People go!"**

Leader # 2: continues

- God knew Pharaoh would not let the children of Israel go free.
- To help Pharaoh decide to release the Israelites, God sent judgments upon Egypt.
- We will hear more of those 10 judgments, called "plagues" later, but, for now, we will talk about just one plague, the last one.
- This plague, when carried out, showed how God separated His People Israel and kept them safe, free from all harm.
- At the same time, God initiated the Passover.

Leader # 3:

- This last plague took place on the night before the children of Israel left Egypt, soon to be fully released from slavery to the Egyptians.
- On that night, an angel of death travelled throughout the land of Egypt with an assignment from God to kill every first-born son living in the land of Egypt.
- That angel of death, however, must *pass over* each home that followed God's special instructions for that night.
- Those special instructions included killing a perfect, sacrificial lamb and applying some of its blood upon the top and sides of the doorframe of each Israelite home.

Picture of an Israelite applying blood of the Lamb to the doorposts and lintel of the home.

- Then, during the night when the Angel of death came to Egypt, he passed over every home with the blood of the lamb on the doorframe of the home, and thus, *the first-born son* within that home lived.
- Wherever the blood of the lamb was not placed upon the home, the angel of death entered, and thus, the first-born son within that home died.
- After that night, which God called **Passover**, Pharaoh released the Israelites to leave Egypt and go into the wilderness to worship and serve God.
- With the events of Passover night, the Israelites fully received the promise of God.
- When that promise came true, Israel had spent four hundred and thirty years in Egypt.

Leader # 4:

- Today, as we look back at the Passover, in the light of the New Testament, we recognize that the entire experience of Passover holds a hidden or prophetic picture of Yeshua.
- Tonight, as we walk through the various parts of the Passover Meal, we uncover or reveal that prophetic picture of Yeshua hidden within the feast.

- As we go through this Passover Meal, please keep in mind that we, like the Israelites in Egypt, must trust God and in His plan of life that He prepared for us to receive.
- Just like the Israelites made a choice to apply the blood of the Lamb to their doorposts and lintel and trusted God to save them from harm, we too, must make a choice in our life, a choice we will discuss, later.

Leader # 1:

- God's plan for us includes having a lamb for our household, too.
- We need a lamb to save us from an eternal judgment, the judgment of eternal death, which comes upon all of us as a penalty for our sin, only our lamb is not an animal that we must sacrifice as did the Israelites.
- For now, remember that just as the Israelites found they needed God to save them from death, and in obedience to God's command, applied a lamb's blood to the doorposts and lentil of their home, we too have something to do to escape the death penalty for sin.
- You know, many people think that God never judges sin.
- Others believe God does judge sin, but He uses a balance scale to do so.

- These conclude that if God, when weighing out the deeds of our life, finds that our good deeds weighs more than the bad, God accepts us into heaven, and thus, we have eternal life, having escaped the judgment of eternal death.
- While this sounds good, the Bible tells us this is just not so.
- As we go through the Passover meal, you will discover that "balance scale" idea, although well known throughout the world, simply does not describe the way God looks at things.
- Also, you will see that God's plan to save us from death for it shows up clearly within the prophetic picture of Yeshua in the Passover Meal.

Leader # 2:

- During the first Passover, as just related, the blood of the Lamb marked those who believed in God's protective plan from the angel of death.
- All who chose to follow God's instructions, were saved from the angel of death.
- All those who put the lamb's blood on the doorpost lived.

- Those who did not put the lamb's blood on the doorpost died.

Leader # 3:

- On that first Passover night, each Israelite ate a piece of the Passover lamb, after it had been roasted by fire.
- This shows us another way in which each Israelite took part in the Passover.
- Their part was to obey God's command. God's part was to provide a way of escape for them from Pharaoh's cruel, enslaving rulership and death.
- In the same manner that God made a way for those Israelites who celebrated the first Passover, God made a way for all people, everywhere, to be free from the slavery of sin and its penalty of death.
- God gave us a spotless Passover lamb, Yeshua Ha' Maschiach.[27]
- God, who loves every one of us, invites us, *individually*, to choose and partake of His special Passover Lamb, just as He invited each Israelite to eat of their special Passover Lamb.
- This shows us that each person *must* make a choice to receive salvation from God's Hand.

---

[27] Pronounced *Yah-Shoe-Ah, Hah Ma She-awk*

- In fact, when you think about it, our whole life and everything we do throughout our time on earth, comes from our choices and the consequences that come from those choices.
- Why should our destination in eternity be any different and not require our choice?
- Did you know that not choosing to accept God's plan for us is also a choice? It is a choice that says, no.

Leader # 4:

- Let's look at why the Bible calls Yeshua a spotless lamb.
- Yeshua is a spotless Passover Lamb, firstly because of His virgin birth, as He was born without sin, and secondly, because Yeshua chose to live His whole life without sin.
- In God's eyes, Yeshua lived a perfect life and God proved His great pleasure in Yeshua when He raised Yeshua from the dead, exempting Him from the curse of death, which resulted from sin.
- As we look at the Passover Lamb, Yeshua, and take note of His total sinlessness, including His birth, we can look at our own life.
- We recognize that we cannot live our life without sinning. For everyone sins.

- To live a life without sin means we never offended God, nor committed any offence against another person while we lived our life.
- No matter how much we promise or struggle to live a sinless life, we know we just cannot do it.
- We also know that when we sin, we do not have it in our own power to turn back the clock, undo the mistakes, and erase the penalty sin incurred.
- Even if it happened that we never sinned, because we are human, we still inherit death because it is part of our inheritance from Adam, the father of all humankind.
- This makes quite a dilemma which we cannot solve on our own.
- Like the Israelites, who could not escape their slavery in Egypt, nor break free from Pharaoh's rule, we need God's help to be free of all slavery to sin and from death's rulership.
- We need someone to save us!

Leader # 1:

- Yeshua came to earth as God's answer to what we need to save us, yes, to be the solution to our dilemma caused by sin.

45

- Thus, in Yeshua, we have the help we need to be free from slavery to sin and the curse of death.
- That provision of Yeshua, as our Saviour, is shown in the Passover Meal.
- Also, as we go through this Passover Meal, each one of us receives a choice to receive Him, or to reaffirm our earlier choice to receive Him as Saviour.
- Remember, as each Israelite received and chose to obey God's instructions about the Passover, *they were saved*.
- Likewise, we can receive and obey God's instructions for our own salvation and *choose to be saved*.
- When we trust God for His Provision of Yeshua as our own Passover Lamb, we align with God's plan of Salvation for our own life.
- When we partake of Yeshua as our Saviour, something wonderful happens.
- God takes the entire righteous life of Yeshua, *(remember His life was totally without sin,)* and God gives us that righteousness.
- We now have what we could never attain on our own.
- In God's eyes, then, He sees us in the same way He sees Yeshua: "sinless" and therefore 100% righteous in His Sight.

Leader # 2:

- Once we sin, as has been said, already, we cannot regain our earlier state of innocence. No, our unrighteousness is with us, forever.
- We have but one choice, just like the Israelites had but one choice on that very first Passover: *to trust God and receive His provision.*
- When we make the choice to accept God's Passover Lamb, *in God's eyes,* He separates us from the penalty of death, just like He separated the Israelites from the angel of death.

Leader # 3:

- The Israelites escaped Pharaoh and the slavery he forced upon them.
- Later, God miraculously parted the Red Sea, taking Israel away forever from the Pharaoh and that horrible life they lived in Egypt.
- The Israelites, by God's miraculous hand, enjoyed an exodus into a new life, being totally set free to serve God.
- Once Yeshua, the Passover Lamb, is our Saviour, we, like the Israelites living in Egypt, escape from the cruel rulership and enslavement to sin, and its curse of death.

We now enjoy an exodus into a new life, free to serve God.

- With Yeshua's righteousness in place in our life, remember, God sees us as holy, separated from sin, or "sanctified". Then, He gives us an added bonus: His Holy Spirit, Who lives within us, to help us to live our life in a manner that is pleasing to God.
- The Kiddish Cup or Cup of Sanctification reminds us of what we have just shared.
- Only through God's Passover Lamb, Yeshua, are we totally acceptable to God and thus, brought out from beneath the heavy yoke of sin.
- From then on, we are accepted by God, and He sees us as His adopted child, part of His family.
- Just like the Israelites, who walked through that very first Passover, lived to leave Egypt, and crossed through the Red Sea, believers in Yeshua live eternally, passing from death into life.
- What a beautiful prophetic picture seen here as we remember the Israelites dilemma and God's solution!
- When we understand this and make the same choice as the Israelites to accept God's provided way out, we enjoy an exodus of

our own to a new life, one set apart to live for God.

- We are free to serve God, and just like the Israelites of old, called to be a people separated unto God.

Leader # 4:

- Once we receive Yeshua as our Saviour, our Passover Lamb, God sanctifies or cleanses us. He sets us apart to live a life pleasing to Him.
- Keeping these things in mind, let us pick up this cup of sanctification.
- As we lift it towards heaven, let us say this blessing together, but putting it in the first-person tense:

ALL: Blessed are You, O Lord our God, King of the Universe, Who keeps me in this life and made a way of escape from the slavery of sin, and set me apart or sanctified me for Your Kingdom, to serve You in newness of life.

*** Drink the Kiddish cup ***

GREENS DIPPED IN SALT WATER

Leader # 1:

- Remember, we said that the Israelites applied some of the sacrificial blood of the lamb upon the top and sides of the doorframes of their homes, so the angel of death would not enter.
- They applied that blood by using a tree branch with leaves, known as Hyssop[28], which is commonly found in Egypt.
- Remember that all homes without the blood of the Lamb on the doorposts were visited by the angel of death and every first-born male child died.
- On that night, a great wailing and lamenting arose in Egypt.
- All the people in the homes, without an application of the Lamb's blood, grieved for the loss of their first-born son, including those in the home of Pharaoh.

---

[28] Hyssop is a branch with many soft leaves which, when dipped in blood, acted like a sponge making the Lamb's blood easy to apply to the two doorposts and lentils.

- Thus, the successor to the throne of Egypt was included in the number of death casualties of this horrible plague.
- In contrast to that scene, the Israelites found that in the morning, every firstborn son in their homes marked with Lamb's blood, lived through that dreadful night.

Leader # 2:

- As the Israelites ate their meal on that first Passover evening, before the visit from the angel of death, they did so with their shoes on their feet, their staff in their hand indicating they were ready to leave Egypt.
- That action spoke of their readiness to say goodbye to the control of Pharaoh, the bitterness of slavery, and the tears shed from the pain of being in bondage to a cruel slave owner.
- Passover celebrates the time of their deliverance, when the blood of the Lamb was applied to the doorposts of the Israelite's home, using hyssop.
- Since that first Passover, as Jews celebrate Passover, they no longer apply the Lamb's blood on the two doorposts and lentil, but they respectfully remember what happened on that first Passover.

- Likewise, for Christians, a lamb's blood is not applied to the doorposts of our home, however, we remember the victory that is ours through the Lamb of God, Yeshua, and the blood He shed for us.
- We remember the bitterness of slavery to sin and those still caught in its grasp.
- We, like the Jews today, represent the hyssop, with a piece of parsley.
- We dip that parsley into a bowl of salt water, symbolizing the tears of slavery, for slavery is cruel and brings many tears with its pain and sorrow.
- As we dip the parsley into the salt water, we remember the pain of a life of those, who *through their own choice,* reject God's plan and thus are excluded from God's presence and will live in darkness for all eternity.

Leader # 3:

- In the Jewish home, traditionally, they remember the tears of their ancestors who lived in Egypt and were enslaved by the Pharaoh.
- Believers in Yeshua, remember the sad state of those who, at this point in their life, do not yet know Yeshua as Messiah and are trapped, living a life of slavery to sin and its bitter end, which is death.

- We also remember those who think there is no hope in the world, some who perhaps have never even heard the message of salvation.
- Together, let us pick up the Parsley, dip it into the salt water.
- Say along with me:

ALL: Blessed are You, O Lord our God, the God of Abraham, Isaac and Jacob, Who gave me this Passover. After I personally accept Yeshua as my Passover Lamb, His blood is applied upon my life. By faith, therefore, in Yeshua, I am free from the slavery of sin and its penalty of death. I have eternal life.

*** Eat the parsley ***

Leader # 4:

- REMEMBER: God gave "a lamb for every household", and so, this means God's plan of Salvation includes every person and their families.
- Let us take a moment, remember those you know who are not yet in Messiah, (not yet saved) and as you pray for their salvation, remember that by faith, all your family

53

members are saved, and their salvation will
be realized one day[29]!
- Pray believing for their salvation!

*(Give some time for each person to silently pray, or if you
prefer, have one person pray for the salvation of others.)*

---

[29] "And they said, "believe on the Lord Jesus Christ, and thou shalt
be saved, and thy house." Acts 16:31.

????

THE 4 QUESTIONS

Leader # 4: continues

- God commanded Israel to remember that first Passover and to teach their children about it throughout all generations.
- To make the learning fun, the Jews established a tradition where the children ask the parents questions about the Passover Meal.
- The questions centred on this theme: *Why is this (Passover) night different from all the other nights when we eat an evening meal together?*
- Throughout the Passover Meal, the traditions answered the questions about the Passover.
- New Testament believers understand the Passover Meal concealed Yeshua, and so, we will ask the same questions as the Jews, but rather than answer them throughout the meal, we will answer each question after it is asked, and then we will better understand

the tradition that became part of the
Passover Meal

Leader # 1:

(Check to see if any children present, or another person was appointed to ask the question.)

QUESTION # 1:	
?	**On all other nights, we eat bread made with yeast, or we may eat matzah. Why, on this night, do we eat only Matzah?**

Leader # 1: continues

- This night is very different. It is a special night chosen by God.
- We eat only Matzah bread because we make this bread without yeast or leaven.
- Yeshua taught us that leaven, or yeast represents sin, so bread made without leaven, represents a life without sin.
- Yeshua never sinned and Yeshua said that He was that bread of Life who came down from heaven.
- Eating unleavened bread helps us to understand and remember these things about Yeshua.
- Tonight, we remember that Yeshua, God incarnate, veiled Himself in flesh and dwelt

with man, and tonight we
remember His sinless life.
- Let's all take a piece of
unbroken Matzah bread and
hold it in our hand.

*** Hold an unbroken piece of Matzah bread in your hand ***

- Do *not* break it & do *not* eat it just yet!
- As you hold the unbroken piece of Matzah
bread in your hand, say this prayer with me:

ALL: Blessed are You, O Lord our God, King of the
Universe, Who gave me the Living Son of God,
Yeshua, the Sinless Passover Lamb, Who came to
earth and lived amongst mankind. Thank You,
Father, for Yeshua, the true bread of Life.

*** Put the unbroken piece of matzah back onto your plate ***

(Remember that matzah, made without leaven, speaks of the sinless life and perfect holiness of Yeshua)

Leader # 2:

(Check to see if any children present, or another person was appointed to ask the question.)

QUESTION # 2:	
?	**On all other nights, we eat all sorts of vegetables. Why on this night do we eat only bitter herbs?**

Leader # 2: continues

On this night, this special night, we must remember:

- The Israelites underwent great hardships and pain when they were in slavery and the bitter herbs remind us of the bitterness of slavery.
- Tonight, we remember the bitter suffering of Yeshua as He, even though sinless, became sin in God's eyes just for our salvation.
- A whip tore His flesh.
- His head was crowned with thorns.
- His hands and feet were nailed to a cross.
- Yet, He did it all for us because He loved us and desired that we be free from the slavery of sin and the penalty of sin which is an eternal life without God.
- He became sin that we might become free from the slavery of sin, and its penalty, death.

Picture of crown of thorns, hammer, and nails
possibly used at the time of Yeshua's death.

- All it takes for us is the acceptance of His Work on the cross, knowing He did it for each one of us, for you and for me.
- Also, we remember that by the stripes (or whipping of Yeshua), we were healed from all forms of sickness, disease, infirmity, pain, grief, and sorrow.

59

- Yeshua took care of these things and more for us. We only need believe it and receive it.
- Together let us pick up the unbroken Matzah bread, one more time.
- Pick up the **unbroken** Matzah bread.

***   **Break it into 2 pieces *****

- As we do this, remember that Yeshua's body was broken for you.
- Shortly, we will dip one of the broken pieces of Matzah into the bitter herbs, and then eat it.
- When you do eat it, you will find it tastes bitter.
- Let that bitterness remind you that Yeshua tasted the bitterness of death on your behalf, taking all punishment for sin, both yours and mine.
- Together, let us dip the matzah.

*** Take one of the broken pieces of Matzah & Dip it in the bitter herb. ***

• Say this along with me:

ALL: Blessed are You, O Lord our God, King of the Universe, Who gave me the Sinless Passover Lamb, Yeshua. Thank You that He took all my sin upon Himself and tasted the bitterness of death, so that I do not have to taste eternal death.

*** Eat the matzah dipped in the bitter herb ***

Leader # 3:
(Check to see if any children present, or another person was appointed to ask the question.)

Question # 3	
?	**On all other nights, we do not dip our foods, no not even once. Why on this night do we dip our food twice?**

Leader # 3: continues

• On this special night, the bittersweet herb reminded the people of Israel of the bitterness of a life of slavery and of their cry to God, until He set them free on that first Passover.

- As believers in Yeshua, we dip the Matzah into the bittersweet herb and we remember both the bitterness of slavery to sin, and of sin's end, which is death, and how Yeshua died in our place to set us free.

- Yeshua, our Passover Lamb, was crucified, and dipped into death, and then dipped into a tomb within the earth, where His body lay for three full days and three full nights.

- When we lift the Matzah up again from the dip, we remember that He victoriously arose from the dead, for because of His sinless life, the grave could not hold Him. Remember also, that all who believe in Yeshua have Eternal Life because, on our behalf, Yeshua took care of eternal death.

- Shortly, we will take the remaining broken piece of Matzah bread on your plate, dip it into the bittersweet herbs and eat it.

- As you taste the dip, and notice both the bitter and sweet taste, remember it symbolizes Yeshua's death and His Glorious Resurrection from the dead.

*** Pick up the second piece of Matzah ***

1. Dip it once into the bitter herb &

2. Dip it once into the bitter-sweet herb

Say this with me:

ALL: Blessed are You, O Lord our God, King of the Universe, Who gave me the Sinless Passover Lamb, Yeshua. Thank You that His sinless life which meant that death had no power over Him. Through resurrection power He arose from the dead, conquering the grave. He did this, that I might walk in newness of life.

*** Eat the matzah dipped twice ***

Leader # 4:

QUESTION # 4:	
?	On all other nights, we sit or recline at the dinner table, but tonight we are only to recline? Why?

Leader # 4: continues

- In ancient times, people that lived in freedom ate their meals reclining at a table that was only slightly elevated off the floor.
- *All the slaves stood up* to eat their meals, and immediately after eating, they went back to work.
- Today, our lifestyle is very different. Our tables are built much higher off the floor than ancient tables; nevertheless, we do not wish to forget the important message in this question.
- We are grateful for our freedom in Messiah, for we live as "free people", removed from the power of darkness, and translated into the kingdom of God's dear Son.
- In addition, there is also another special message in the act of reclining:
- Believers in Messiah "Rest" in what God did, on our behalf, through Yeshua.
- We rest from all our efforts to gain God's approval.
- We rest from all works of the flesh, which we think, may please God.
- We stop doing our own thing and embrace the things that God asks of us.

Take a moment, relax in your chair, and take a deep breath

- As you do that, remember to rest in the fact that, with Yeshua as your Saviour, you have God's approval.
- To choose Yeshua as your Saviour is to accept the work done by God, through Yeshua.
- Doing so, means that you entered God's rest in the area of your salvation, not expecting to get to heaven because of the sum of your good works.
- The Israelites, who exited Egypt and arrived at the Promised Land, had opportunity to enter God's rest, however, not all did so.
- *Hebrews 3:17 to 19 tells us that generation of Israelites, apart from two leaders, named Caleb and Joshua, never entered the Promised land because they failed to enter God's rest.*
- God was grieved with Israel for 40 years because those Israelites refused to see God as bigger and mightier than the problems that they faced in following God's plan to obtain Canaan Land.
- That exodus generation never entered God's rest, since they never believed God to fulfil His Word to them.

- All but the two faithful leaders (Joshua and Caleb), died in the wilderness, never reaching their destiny of the Promised Land.
- We are told to remember their mistake, their failure to rest in God's abilities to help them.
- We are told not to behave like they did, living in unbelief.
- However, when we believe, accepting the works God did for us, we enter God's rest, and then we live out our lives from that point of rest.
- That rest is a very important aspect of our faith.
- To remember that aspect, to express our trust in God, say this with me, *resting comfortably in your chair:*

ALL: Blessed are You, O Lord our God, King of the Universe, Who gave me the Sinless Passover Lamb, Yeshua. Through Yeshua, You brought me out from beneath the power of darkness and translated me into the Kingdom of Your dear Son. I take my rest in the works Yeshua did on the cross, ever grateful for Your provision of my salvation through Yeshua Ha' Maschiach.

THE CUP OF JUDGMENT

Leader # 1:

- Think with me, back to the time of the very first Passover, when the Israelites were still in Egypt and God commanded Pharaoh, **"Let My People go!"**

ALL: Let My People Go!

- Pharaoh resisted God's orders and so, to help him obey God's command, the Lord sent 10 specific judgments or plagues.
- Before each judgment or plague came, God, through Moses, announced their coming in Pharaoh's hearing.
- When that plague came, the false gods of Egypt, in which the people trusted to protect them, were shown as impotent and unable to stand against the power of the God of Abraham, Isaac and Jacob.
- As the plague did not touch the Israelites, Pharaoh and the Egyptians could see God's protective hand rested upon the Israelites.

- Egyptians saw that through God's mighty hand to protect Israel, the God of Israel fought Israel's cause for freedom from slavery.
- Each Egyptian could see that the false gods in which they trusted, could not oppose the strength of the true God, nor His Arm of power which affected the real world, and thus, brought about His promised deliverance to the Israelites.
- Pharaoh too would know that the Egyptian gods, in which he trusted, were powerless against the true God, Who commanded him to let His People go. That recognition should cause him to obey the Lord, thus releasing the Israelites to leave Egypt.

Leader # 2:

- For centuries, at each Passover gathering, from the first Passover onwards, the children of Israel recalled the ten plagues that God sent to Egypt to free them from slavery.
- Yearly, during the Passover meal, they would name the plague, and as they did, each person would take a drop of wine from their cup. They then put that drop of wine on a plate, grateful for the plague from which they were spared, including the last

plague, when every first-born son was spared from death.

- Later, some Jews chose not to remember the 10 plagues in Egypt, preferring to think instead about the 10 commandments they received from God at Mount Sinai.

- God's own finger wrote the 10 commandments upon two tablets of stone, and God gave them to Moses when he was with God, upon Mount Sinai.

- These 10 commandments showed Israel how to live a pleasing life before God in the Promised Land.

- After having received the stone tablets, Moses returned from Mt. Sinai, but as he approached the Israelite camp, he found the people worshipping a golden idol fashioned after a calf.

- They proclaimed that this was the 'god' that brought them out of Egypt.

- Moses, in anger, threw those stone tablets to the ground, breaking them in pieces, thus symbolizing that all humanity will break God's commandments.

- On that same day, due to their idolatry, God's judgment hit hard, and three thousand people died.

- At this Passover Meal, we honour the Sinless One, Yeshua, who kept all God's commandments. We thus recall the Ten Commandments that Yeshua fulfilled, but all humanity fails to keep.

- Furthermore, we remember that God made Yeshua, Who knew no sin, to be sin for us, that we might be made the righteousness of God in Him.

Leader # 3:

- Tonight, as **we read** the 10 commandments, remember that these came from God's Heart of Love to His people, who were to treat each other with love and respect.
- As you hear each commandment read, take your finger, dip it into the wine, and then remove your finger from the cup, and dab the drop of wine that is on your finger onto the plate in front of you.
- As you do that, think about that commandment in which God calls us to love God above all things and our neighbour as ourselves.
- Conversely, think how difficult it is to keep that commandment in its entirety, all the time, in every circumstance and in every situation of life.
- Let us read the 10 commandments together, noting those who apply directly to God, and

those that apply to our behaviour towards others.

THE TEN COMMANDMENTS

Our Behaviour towards God:

1   I am the LORD your God. I brought you out of the land of Egypt, out of the house of slavery. You shall put no other gods before Me.

2   You shall not make for yourselves any carved image, or any likeness of anything that is in heaven above, or that is in the earth beneath, or that is in the water under the earth.

3   You shall not take the name of the LORD your God in vain; for the LORD will not hold anyone guiltless who takes His Holy name in vain.

71

4 Remember the Sabbath day, to keep it holy. Six days you shall work hard and do all your labours, but the seventh day is the Sabbath of the LORD your God and on that day, you shall not do any work. Neither you, nor your son or daughter, nor your male or female servants, nor your cattle, nor the stranger that is within your gates shall labour, for in six days the LORD made heaven and earth, the sea, and everything in them, and then He rested the seventh day: wherefore the LORD blessed the Sabbath day and set it apart.

Our behaviour towards others:

5 Respect your father and your mother so that your days may be long upon the land which the LORD your God gives you.

6 You shall not kill.

7 You shall not commit adultery.

8 You shall not steal.

9 You shall not bear false witness against your neighbour.

10 You shall not covet your neighbour's house; you shall not covet your neighbour's wife, or his male or female servants, or his ox, or his ass, or anything that belongs to your neighbour.

Leader # 3: continues

- When a person breaks a commandment, they sin, and thus, become bound to that sin and subject to God's judgment.
- That judgment is eternal death, which means to live in everlasting darkness without God.
- All those, however, who trust in Messiah, are set free from that slavery to sin and from the penalty of death. They won't suffer an eternity away from God.
- Yeshua made all that possible when He became sin for us. He then went to the cross, and there, took upon Himself our punishment, our judgment for all our failures.
- We remember that Yeshua, the Passover Lamb, died in our place, drinking the cup of Judgment for all those who believe in Him.
- With a grateful heart, let us thank God for Yeshua
- Raise your cup towards heaven and say with me:

ALL: Blessed are You, O Lord our God, King of the Universe, Who designed me to love You with all my heart, mind, soul and strength; and to love my neighbour as I love myself.

Thank You that, even though I often failed in keeping Your commandments and thus deserved Your just punishment, You provided Yeshua, the perfect Passover Lamb, to take that punishment for me and die in my place.

With thankfulness for Yeshua, I drink this cup.

*** Drink the cup of Judgment***

PARTAKE OF THE LAMB

(At this part of the meal, have a person get ready to distribute some cooked lamb for the people to eat).

Leader # 4:

- God gave specific instructions about the Passover Lamb, of which, the people of God would partake. The lamb must be perfect, with no defects, such as a broken leg, or injury of any kind.
- Once the Israelites carefully chose their lamb, which they inspected to ensure it met with God's requirements, they then took the lamb to their house, thus removing the lamb from the remainder of the herd.
- The chosen lamb then lived in the Israelite home for four days, never allowed to go back to its family or familiar surroundings.

- It must remain within the Israelite's home, where family members cared for and loved it.
- On the fourth day, as the father led the lamb out of the house to the slaughter, the lamb went willingly, without uttering a peep.
- After the father butchered the lamb, it was roasted and then each person ate a portion of that Lamb.

Leader # 1:

- Yeshua, God's Perfect Lamb was chosen by God, our Father. He was found without blemish in God's eyes, thus meeting all of God's requirements.
- When Yeshua went to the cross, He first was separated from all his friends and loved ones.
- He stood before King Herod, the court of the Jews and the governor of Rome, Pontius Pilate.
- He was flogged, crowned with thorns, and then crucified.
- Yeshua was as a lamb led willingly to the slaughter, uttering not a peep.
- Tonight, we recall Yeshua, God's Perfect Passover Lamb, in appreciation for all He did for us.

- Each person present also eats a piece of lamb to signify that each one must personally accept the Salvation done on their behalf.

Leader # 2::

- Please pass out the lamb. When everyone has a piece of lamb in his or her hand, we will eat together.
- Let us now lift the lamb before the Lord.
- Say this with me.

ALL: Blessed are You, O Lord our God, King of the Universe, Who gave me Yeshua, the Passover lamb. Today, as I eat this piece of Lamb, I realize that Yeshua met all Your requirements as the perfect Passover Lamb, without blemish. Just as the Israelites, individually chose to eat their Passover lamb, I realize that I must personally choose to accept Yeshua as my Saviour.

*** Eat piece of lamb together ***

WASHING THE HANDS[30]

(Preparation Instructions: Have some people available to put warm water into jugs, prepare the basins for washing and towelettes for drying the hands.)

Leader # 3:

- On the night before Yeshua died, during the Passover before the cross, scripture tells us that Yeshua rose from supper, laid aside His garments, and took a towel and wrapped it around Himself.
- Then He poured water into a basin and began to wash the feet of the disciples, but when He came to Peter, Peter refused to allow Yeshua to wash his feet.
- John 13:8-11 says,
  "Peter said unto him, You shall never wash my feet.

---

[30] Some believers prefer to do this, and then, after the meal, do a foot washing, as it was after the meal, John 13:4, that Yeshua washed feet. If you intend to do this, let your guests know before they come so they can come prepared, e.g. wear appropriate foot socks, nylons, etc.

- Yeshua answered him, If I wash you not, you have no part with me.
- Simon Peter said unto him, Lord, not my feet only, but also my hands and my head.
- Yeshua said to him, He that is washed needs only to wash his feet but is clean in every way: and you are clean, but not all. For he knew who should betray him; therefore, said he, 'You are not all clean".

Leader # 4:

- John 13:12-17 tells us even more about this time of washing the disciple's feet:
- "So, after Yeshua had washed their feet, and had taken his garments, and sat back down again, He said unto His Disciples, do you know what I have done to you?"
- "You call me Master and Lord: and you say well; for so I am. If I then, your Lord and Master, have washed your feet; you also ought to wash one another's feet."
- "For I have given you an example, that you should do as I have done to you."
- "Verily, verily, I say unto you, the servant is not greater than his lord; neither he that is sent greater than he that sent him. If you know these things, happy are you if ye do them."

Leader # 1::

- Yeshua is God's Servant Who came to benefit and serve man, and in perfect humility, washed the disciple's feet.
- Though Yeshua washed His disciple's feet after the supper, at this point, we will wash our hands before eating our meal, since doing so has long been a standing practice of cleanliness.
- However, the point we do it here, is to primarily remember Yeshua's humility in loving and caring for others and His desire to serve.
- In a like mind, we therefore, serve our neighbour, pouring the water over their hands, showing our care for them.
- As we do this, we remember that caring for our neighbour every day, is not just washing their hands on Passover, but also lovingly bringing the gospel of salvation to everyone and praying for them, too.
- It is showing that we care for their quality of life on this earth as they live it now, and for their future life as they leave this life for eternity.

(Give instructions for washing the hands.)

80

THANKSGIVING FOR MAIN MEAL[31].

Leader # 1: continues

- Let us give thanks to the Lord for the meal which we are about to eat.
- Say this with me:

ALL: Blessed are you, O Lord our God, King of the Universe, Who provides for me continually, and on this night has given me this Passover Meal. Thank You, Lord, for every person gathered at this table. May Your covenant blessings come upon each one here tonight, as well as all their loved ones and friends whom they cherish as dear.

(Give instructions on how to proceed to eat the meal.)

---

[31] The Bible teaches that after you have eaten and are full, you give thanks. In the Jewish mindset, to pray before a meal is not a blessing but rather a thanksgiving. They think this way because all that God made was good, and therefore the food is already blessed.

[32] It takes about an hour to come to this point in the Passover meal. In preparing your food. This gives you a ballpark figure about what time your food should be cooked by and ready to eat.

81

SECTION 3

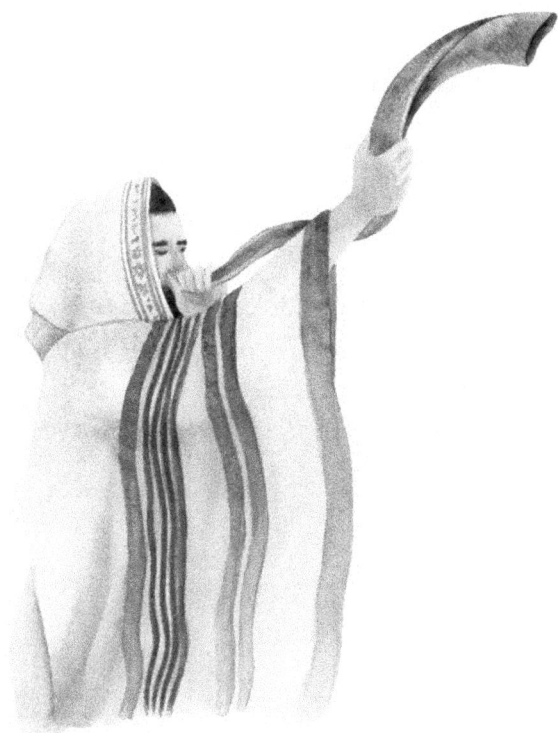

PASSOVER
CELEBRATION
(Part 2)

Remember: *After the meal, as you continue with the Passover Celebration, you share the last 2 cups. If you did not set out 4 cups for each person, but rather chose to refill one cup throughout the meal, ensure in cleaning up your table, your guests are left with a cup from which to drink the last 2 cups.*

ELIJAH'S COMING

Leader # 1:

- It is a custom of the Jewish believers to go to the door and to look for Elijah, to see if he will arrive at this Passover.
- For New Covenant believers, we know that, according to Yeshua's words, John the Baptist walked in the spirit and power of Elijah.
- We therefore hold another mindset. Since it is 2000 plus years after the cross, instead we look for Messiah's Second Coming, which, of course, will first be preceded by the spirit of Elijah.
- This spirit brings repentance, and so, expressing our faith in God's word we might wish to send one person to
- Go to the door and open it, look for Elijah, then return to the gathering.
- Thank YeHoVaH for His promise to send the Spirit of Elijah before the great and terrible day of the LORD.
- Look forward to that coming and the reaping of the end time harvest.
- Sing a song, here, if you wish, perhaps Days of Elijah.

85

THE BREAD OF REDEMPTION

Leader # 2:

- From our earlier comments, you know that this bread is unleavened and thus depicts Messiah's life without sin.
- Notice also, there are stripes and holes in this bread.
- These remind us of the whip marks Yeshua received in His Body.
- In fact, to take this communion is to recognize that His Body was broken for you that you may enjoy healing.
- All who have accepted the Messiah as their personal Saviour are invited to partake of this Matzah bread.

Leader # 3:

- 1 Cor. 11: 23-29 says.
  For I have received of the Lord that which also I delivered unto you, that Yeshua, on the same night in which he was betrayed, took unleavened bread, symbolizing His sinless[33] body. And when he had given thanks, He broke it, and said, Take,

---

[33] The word sinless added by author.

eat, this is my body, which is broken for you: this do in remembrance of me."

"After supper, in the same manner, Yeshua also took the cup, saying, "This cup is the cup of the New Covenant in my blood: this you do, for as often as you drink it, do so, in remembrance of me. For as often as you eat this bread, and drink this cup, you show the Lord's death until He comes".

"Wherefore, whosoever shall eat this bread, and drink this cup of the Lord, unworthily, shall be guilty of the body and blood of the Lord. But let a person examine themselves, and then, let him eat of that bread, and drink of that cup. For he that eats and drinks unworthily, eats and drinks damnation to themselves, not discerning the Lord's body".

- We will give you some time now to reflect upon your life, examining yourself as the scriptures admonish us.

(Give some time before saying the prayer)

Leader # 4:

- Say this with me:

ALL: Blessed are You, O Lord our God, King of the Universe, Who gave me this bread from Heaven, the bread of life, this bread of Redemption, which is the bread of Your Only Son Yeshua. I partake of this bread understanding that, by Yeshua's stripes, I was healed.

*** Eat bread of Redemption together ***

THE CUP OF REDEMPTION

Leader # 4: continues

- In the very same manner, Yeshua took the Cup of Redemption
- He said the blessing over it and passed it among His disciples, saying to them, "This is the cup of the New Covenant, sealed with His Blood".
- He then said, "Do this[34] in remembrance of Me!"

We remember as He commanded:

- The Passover and what it entailed, and why.
- The Cup from which Yeshua drank for our Redemption.
- The price He willingly paid for us.
- The Healing He brought about for us, so we may be whole in body, mind, soul, and spirit.

---

[34] Messianic believers interpret this to mean, do this, *the Passover*, in remembrance of Me, since Yeshua fulfilled that feast with His Life and sacrificial death. Of course, breaking bread daily meant a reminder of this great gift that Yeshua paid for each one.

- The removing of sin, its penalty, and the cleansing of our conscience.
- All of which He did for you and for me.

Leader # 1:

- 1 John 1:7 tells us *"But if we walk in the light, as he is in the light, we have fellowship one with another, and the blood of Yeshua Ha' Maschiach, His Son, cleanses us from all sin."*
- Say this with me:

ALL: Blessed are You, O Lord our God, King of the Universe, Who gave me this New Covenant through Your Only Son Yeshua. Thank You, Lord, for Your forgiveness and such a great salvation. As I partake of this Cup of Redemption, I acknowledge that, according to Your Word, Yeshua Ha' Maschiach, through His precious blood, made complete atonement for my sin. He took the penalty on my behalf, and now I am free to live my life serving You. Thank You that I am redeemed!

*** Drink the cup of redemption***

THE CUP OF PRAISE

Leader # 1: continues

- This Cup, remember, comes from Exodus 6:7 which quotes the Lord who said, *"I will take you to Myself, for a people and I will be to you a God"*.

- Matthew 26: 28-30 tells us of an important fact. Yeshua said, *"For this is my blood of the New Testament, which is shed for many for the remission of sins. But I say unto you, I will not drink henceforth of this fruit of the vine, until that day when I drink it new with you in my Father's kingdom. And when they had sung a hymn, they went out into the mount of Olives"*.

- We know from this comment, that after Yeshua drank the Cup of Redemption, **He did not drink the next cup which is the cup of Praise.**

- This cup He will drink with His Bride at the marriage supper of the Lamb.

- So, now we will say" The Great Hallel" and **come back to this cup, shortly.**

91

THE GREAT HALLEL

Leader # 1: continues

- In Jewish tradition, for centuries, while Israel had their temple, Psalms 113 to 118 was either sung or recited as the Passover Lamb was slain in the temple.
- These same Psalms were also either sung or recited on the night of Passover by individual families as they gathered in their homes for Passover.
- We call this compilation of songs, "the Great Hallel".
- Since these Psalms were recited, or perhaps even sung, when the Temple in Israel stood, we know Yeshua and His disciples during their lifetime recited or sang them, and *perhaps*, this was the song they sang as mentioned in Matthew 26:30 before Yeshua went to the cross.
- Unfortunately, some of the ancient tunes have been lost and so, tonight, we will only read these Psalms.
- As we read the Great Hallel, let us remember that these very words rang from the lips of

our Savour during His lifetime upon this earth, even on His lips, knowing He was about to die a horrible death on the cross, for He knew this, long before the night before His crucifixion.

- Please listen carefully to the instructions on how we will read the Great Hallel.

- This part of the Passover Meal happens still, while we are all at the table.

- Each person has an opportunity to take their turn reading the leader's part, while the rest of us read the response.

- I will start first, and then, the person next to me, on my right will take the leadership, then the person on their right after them, and so on and so forth until we are finished all the Psalms.

- Remember, whenever you see the Word LORD, we will say YeHoVaH. [35]

---

[35] If you do not plan on doing this, then leave this line out.

THE GREAT HALLEL

PSALM 113	
Leader	Praise the LORD. Oh, all His servants, Praise the LORD, yes, praise the name of the LORD.
ALL	Blessed be the name of the LORD from this time forth and for evermore.
Leader	From sunrise to sunset, the LORD'S Name is to be praised.
ALL	The LORD is high above all nations, and His glory above the heavens.
Leader	Who is like unto the LORD our God, Who dwells on high,
ALL	Who humbles Himself to look into the things that are in heaven, and in the earth! He raises up the poor out of the dust, and lifts the needy out of the dunghill;
Leader	That He may set him with princes, even with the princes of his people.
ALL	He makes the barren woman to keep house, and to be a joyful mother of children. Praise the LORD!

PSALM 114	
Leader	When Israel went out of Egypt, the house of Jacob from a people of foreign language;

94

ALL	Judah was his sanctuary, and Israel his dominion.
Leader	The sea saw it and fled: Jordan was driven back.
ALL	The mountains skipped like rams, and the little hills like lambs.
Leader	What troubled you, O you sea, that you fled? you Jordan, that you were driven back?
ALL	You mountains that you skipped like rams; and you little hills, like lambs?
Leader	Tremble, you earth, at the presence of the Lord, at the presence of the God of Jacob;
ALL	Who turned the rock into a standing water, the flint into a fountain of waters.

PSALM 115

Leader	Not unto us, O LORD, not unto us, but unto Your Name give glory, for Your mercy, and for Your Truth's sake.
ALL	Wherefore should the heathen say, "Where is now their God?"
Leader	But our God is in the heavens: He has done whatsoever He has pleased.
ALL	Their idols are silver and gold, the work of men's hands.
Leader	They have mouths, but they speak not: eyes have they, but they see not:

ALL	They have ears, but they hear not: noses have they, but they smell not:
Leader	They have hands, but they handle not: feet have they, but they walk not: neither do they speak through their throat.
ALL	Those that make them are like them and so is everyone that trusts in them.
Leader	O Israel, trust in the LORD: He is your help and shield.
ALL	O house of Aaron, trust in the LORD: He is your help and shield.
Leader	All you that fear the LORD, trust in the LORD: He is your help and shield.
ALL	The LORD remembered us: He will bless us; He will bless the house of Israel; He will bless the house of Aaron. He will bless all those that fear the LORD, both small and great.
Leader	The LORD shall increase you more and more, you and your children.
ALL	You are blessed of the LORD, which made heaven and earth.
Leader	The heaven, yes even the heavens, are the LORD'S: but the earth He has given to the children of men.
ALL	The dead do not praise the LORD; neither does anyone that go down into the silence of death.

Leader	But we will bless the LORD from this time forth and for evermore.
ALL	Praise the LORD

PSALM 116

Leader	I love the Lord, for He has heard my voice. He heard my cry for mercy.
ALL	Because He turned His ear to me, I will call on Him as long as I live.
Leader	The sorrows of death entangled me, the anguish of hell and the grave came upon me; trouble and sorrow overcame me.
ALL	Then I called upon the name of the Lord: "O Lord save me and deliver me!"
Leader	Gracious is the LORD, and righteous; yes, our God is merciful.
ALL	The LORD preserves those open to His will: I was brought low, and He helped me.
Leader	Be at rest, O my soul, for the Lord has dealt wonderfully with me.
ALL	The Lord has delivered my soul from death, my eyes from tears, and my feet from falling. Now I will walk before the LORD in the land of the living.
Leader	I believed, therefore have I spoken. I was greatly afflicted: I said in my haste, All men are liars. What shall I give unto the

LORD to repay Him for all his benefits toward me?

ALL   I will take the Cup of Salvation and call upon the name of the LORD. I will pay my vows unto the LORD now in the presence of all his people.

Leader   Precious in the sight of the LORD is the death of his saints. O LORD, truly I am thy servant; I am thy servant, and the son of Your handmaid: You have broken the chains of slavery.

ALL   I will offer to You the sacrifice of thanksgiving, and I will call upon the name of the LORD.

Leader   I will pay my vows unto the LORD now in the presence of all his people, in the courts of the LORD'S house, in the midst of thee, O Jerusalem.

ALL   Praise the LORD.

PSALM 117

Leader   O praise the LORD, all the nations of the earth: praise Him, all the people.

ALL   His merciful kindness is great toward us: and the truth of the LORD endures forever. Praise the LORD.

PSALM 118

Leader	O give thanks unto the LORD, for He is good: because His mercy endures forever.
ALL	Let Israel now say, that His mercy endures for ever
Leader	Let the house of Aaron now say, that His mercy endures forever.
ALL	Let all that fear the LORD say that His mercy endures forever.
Leader	I called upon the LORD in distress: the LORD answered me, and set me in a large place, He set me free.
ALL	The LORD is on my side; I will not fear: what can man do unto me?
Leader	The LORD takes my part with them that help me: therefore, shall I walk in triumph over all those that hate me. It is better to trust in the LORD than to put my confidence in man.
ALL	It is better to trust in the LORD than to put confidence in princes. All nations compassed me about: but in the name of the LORD, they will be cut off. They compassed me about; yes, they compassed me about: but in the name of the LORD I will cut them off.
Leader	They compassed me about like bees; they died out as quickly as thorns burned in a

	fire; in the name of the LORD I will cut them off.
ALL	I was pushed back, and I was ready to fall, but the LORD helped me.
Leader	The LORD is my strength and song, and He has become my salvation. The voice of rejoicing and salvation is in the tabernacles of the righteous: the right hand of the LORD doeth courageously.
ALL	The right hand of the LORD is high: the right hand of the LORD doeth mighty things.
Leader	I shall not die, but live, and declare the works that God has done for me, the mighty works of the LORD.
ALL	The LORD hath chastened me but He did not give me over to death.

THE CUP OF PRAISE CONTINUED

Leader # 2:

- When we are in Messiah, we are part of Yeshua's body on earth, which is made up of redeemed Jews and Gentiles, which the Apostle Paul called "The One New Man".
- Another title to which we often refer is "the Bride of Messiah".
- As we conclude this Passover meal, we are going to remember the unity of all those in Messiah and think about the Wedding Supper of the Lamb in which Yeshua will drink this cup with His Bride.
- As we lift this Cup of Praise to the Lord, we thank Him deeply, from our hearts, for all that He has done for us.
- We look forward to the marriage supper of the Lamb!
- What a reason to celebrate!
- Say this along with me:

ALL: Blessed are You, O Lord our God, King of the Universe, Who gave me the fruit of the vine and the Passover Lamb. Thank you for translating me out of the power of darkness and placing me in the kingdom of God. Thank You that, through Yeshua, You are my God, and I belong to You! For Your Great

Act of Mercy and Redemption, and for the future Marriage Supper of the Lamb, I praise You!

*** Drink the cup of Praise ***

(At this point, the Leader Rotation ends, and Leader # 1 concludes.)

Leader # 1:

- Throughout the meal tonight, as you walked through this Passover celebration with us, you have heard the gospel message.
- As you can see, Yeshua paid a great price for you and for me, so we'd be free from sin and receive Eternal Life.
- However, like the Israelite who, on that first Passover, had a choice to apply the blood of the lamb on the doorposts, or die exposed to the angel of death, each person, in their lifetime, must make a choice to receive the works Yeshua did on their behalf.
- We'd like to give you an opportunity to do that now, so as this meal concludes, we'd like to give you a moment to think about accepting Yeshua's invitation. Then, we'll pray a prayer together.
- If you pray this prayer for the first time in your life, it is the beginning of a new life for

you, and after the meal, we'd like to speak with you further to help you understand.
- While a person need only say this prayer once, so as not to embarrass anyone and single them out, we will all say this prayer together.

(Give a minute here for your guests to consider this.)

ALL: "Heavenly Father, I acknowledge before You that I am a sinner and the punishment for my sins sentenced me to a life without God for all eternity. Thank You for sending Yeshua to the earth to die in my place, to take my punishment and to make it possible for me to live eternally. I believe You raised Yeshua from the dead, and once I accept Him as my personal Saviour, forsaking my sins, my old life dies and my new life begins.

Tonight, I humbly ask You to forgive me of my sins, and I take Yeshua Ha' Maschiach as my personal Saviour, as my own Passover Lamb. I open my heart to receive the works of the cross You provided for me & with Your help, I will now live my life with You as Lord and Master of my life. Help me to live my life, from this point onward, differently, in a manner pleasing to You." Amen

Leader # 1:

- If you prayed this prayer for the first time, tonight, and meant it, please speak to me or another group leader.
- We ask this for two reasons: first, the Bible says we must confess with our mouth unto salvation, and so it is very important that you tell someone of your commitment. Second, we'd like to ensure that you understand what's happened, and how to take the next steps in your life, to live the fullest life possible, with Yeshua as your Messiah.
- Doing this is very important, for the Bible says a person believes with the heart unto righteousness and confesses with the mouth unto salvation[36].

*** At this point the Passover Meal ends ***

---

[36] In the early church, confessions of faith were followed by water baptism.

FINAL INSTRUCTIONS & CLOSING

(If you left dessert to this part of the Passover Meal, you can bring it out and get things ready such as coffee or tea, or other refreshments at this time.)

It is a good thing to let your guests stay a while and fellowship with each other, if they wish to do so. Please *decide beforehand what you'd prefer to do to end your Passover meal celebration.*

Here are a few suggestions. Use one or more at time permits.

- Ask for testimonies from those at the table, giving them time to say something special, that is on their heart. *(Perhaps what they liked best about the Passover celebration.)*
- Ask people the following question and let them discuss the answer. "If you, like the Egyptians, prepared to leave a country in which you have lived for a time, and knew you would not come back, what 1 thing would you be sure to bring with you?"
- Ask the older ones in the group to give a blessing on the younger people in the group.
- Ask the young children what they liked best on this special night.

Leader # 1 (or Host or Hostess)

Thank your guests for coming.
Make your final announcements.
Close your gathering any way you prefer.

FINAL COMMENT TO THE HOST/HOSTESS

Regarding those who accepted Yeshua as their Saviour this evening, perhaps you might have some information handy for them to read or invite them back to discuss their salvation with them further. Whatever you choose to do, please ensure they are cared for and discipled in the best way you can recommend, either through yourself, a pastor, deacon, or some other way you know will help them.

APPENDIX

APPENDIX

HELPFUL INDEX

A

A Table Ready For Passover 21

E

Elijah's Coming 85

F

Food & Beverage 13

G

Greens Dipped In Salt Water 50

H

Honouring The Name Of God 10

L

Leader Overview 27
Lighting Of The Candle 33

M

Meal Divisions 11

P

Partake Of The Lamb 75
Passover Opening 33

Pre-Celebration Instructions 24
Preliminaries *After* Guests Are Seated 29

R

Recipe For Charoset 23

S

Shofar Blow 30
Suggestions For Picking Leaders 25

T

Table Setting 12
Thanksgiving For 81
The 4 Questions 55
The Bread Of Redemption 86
The Cup Of Judgment 67
The Cup Of Praise 91
The Cup Of Praise Continued 101
The Great Hallel 92
The Haggadah 8
The Kiddish Cup 36
The Ten Commandments 71
This Haggadah Overview 9

W

Washing The Hands 78

OTHER BOOKS BY JEANNE METCALF

Above Artificial Intelligence
Finding God in a World of AI
An Arsenal of Powerful Prayers
Scriptural Prayers to Move Mountains,
Arising Incense
A Believer's Priesthood
Candidate for A Miracle
Wisdom from the miracles of Yeshua
Foundations of Revival
Biblical Evidence for Revival
His Reflection
What God longs to see in His People
Heaven's Greater Government
Behind the Scenes of Earth's Events
In The Name of Yehovah We Set Up Our Banners
Biblical use of banners
It's All About Heaven
As Pictured in Scripture
Kingdom Keys for Kingdom Kids
Walking in Kingdom Power
Molded for the Miraculous
Why God made You!
Releasing the Impossible
The Limitless Power of Intercession
Salvation Depicted in a Meal
Passover Haggadah
The Jeremiah Generation
God's Response to Injustice

The Warrior Bride-
>God's Kingdom Advancing through Spiritual Warfare

Thy Kingdom Come
>Entering God's Rest in Prayer

Watching, Waiting, Warning
>Obeying Yeshua's Command to Watch & Pray

When Nations Rumble
>A Study of the Book of Amos

Worship in Spirit and In Truth
>The Tabernacle of David - Past, Present & Future

I-Stock Pictures Used in this book:

Lamb	1307155638
Lamb meat	134547127
Door Posts with Blood	173739497
Menorah	614983156
Matzah	148579301
Goblet	1475560467
Goblet & Matzah	1314955941
Shofar	1617166336
Shofar man with tallit	1496616184
Crown Underline	1286359176, 1169730276
Music Bar	1459334557
Pitcher and Bowl	922886412
10 Commandments	1084425710
Charoset	470181204
Crown of Thorns, Nails	1290401675
Balance Scale	177635325
Praying Hands	1211534036

ABOUT JEANNE METCALF

Jeanne believes the Word of God opens a door to help every believer to know their God. That knowledge, once gleaned and retained, makes strong believers who then can stand in the real world in which we live.

With these convictions in mind, Jeanne, inspired and led by the Holy Spirit, began to write in the 1990's. Soon she developed inductive style Bible Studies and self-published them for her students to use. With her major goal to equip the saints, she soon discovered that her sound teachings, presented with clarity and simplicity, made an impact. As long as her listeners put in their valuable time to study scripture and took Jeanne's advice to call upon the Holy Spirit to help them, they became powerful believers, transformed, prepared and ready to stand in their generation.

Today, past students who studied the Bible with Jeanne, as well current new students, testify as to the validity of Jeanne's writing and teaching gift. They love the clarity and simplicity of the Word as she presents it in a refreshing straightforward format. Thus, they encouraged Jeanne to make her books more widely available. Therefore, Jeanne began Cegullah Publishing, and then a year later, opened Cegullah Apologetic Academy. The academy, still receiving its early foundations, is one more avenue to present Bible Study material to all who wish to be strong in YeHoVaH and the strength of His might.

A greater availability of Jeanne's works (as well as other authors which Cegullah Publishing looks forward to publishing in the future), opens doors for more people to know their God and do exploits!

"But the people that know their God shall be strong and do exploits". (Daniel 11:32

THANKYOU

In Israel in 2011, I attended my very first Passover celebration in the Galilee. As the Passover meal ended, the leader of that group gave me his basic outline to use for Passover when I returned to Canada. At that time, he told me that he believed God would have me publish a book regarding the Passover celebration sometime down the road. Admittedly, those words went right over my head. Nevertheless, his encouragement to use his few page outline as the bones of a Passover celebration helped tremendously. Over the years, I added the meat to those bones as YeHoVaH led, and today, we have this book which includes many helps and instructions of things I learned to help make the Passover run smoothly and be most memorable to attendees.

This, then, is a thank you to that leader, who preferred to remain anonymous, and for his input into my life regarding the necessities of a Passover meal.

CEGULLAH PUBLISHING,
an integral part of

Visit us and *take advantage of the free information on our website put there to build your faith!*
Listen to prayer podcasts, the Faith Choice Program, and other free helps to build your Christian Faith.

CEGULLAH PUBLISHING & APOLOGETICS ACADEMY.
cegullahpublishing.ca